Pebble® Plus
Bilingüe/Bilingual

Dinosaurios y animales prehistóricos/Dinosaurs and Prehistoric Animals

Alosaurio/Allosaurus

por/by Helen Frost

Traducción/Translation: Dr. Martín Luis Guzmán Ferrer

Editor Consultor/Consulting Editor: Dra. Gail Saunders-Smith

Consultor/Consultant: Jack Horner, Curator of Paleontology
Museum of the Rockies
Bozeman, Montana

Capstone press®

Mankato, Minnesota

Pebble Plus is published by Capstone Press,
151 Good Counsel Drive, P.O. Box 669, Mankato, Minnesota 56002.
www.capstonepress.com

1 2 3 4 5 6 11 10 09 08 07 06

Library of Congress Cataloging-in-Publication Data
Frost, Helen, 1949–
    [Allosaurus. Spanish & English]
    Alosaurio = Allosaurus/de/by Helen Frost.
    p. cm.—(Pebble Plus. Dinosaurios y animales prehistóricos = Pebble Plus. Dinosaurs and
prehistoric animals)
    Includes index.
    ISBN-13: 978-0-7368-6683-5 (hardcover)
    ISBN-10: 0-7368-6683-3 (hardcover)
    1. Allosaurus—Juvenile literature. I. Title: Allosaurus. II. Title. III. Pebble Plus. Dinosaurios y
animales prehistóricos.
QE862.S3F7718 2007
567.912—dc22   2005037474

Summary: Simple text and illustrations present allosaurus, its body parts, and behavior—in both English
    and Spanish.

Editorial Credits
Martha E. H. Rustad, editor; Katy Kudela, bilingual editor; Eida del Risco, Spanish copy editor; Linda Clavel,
    set designer; Jon Hughes, illustrator; Wanda Winch, photo researcher; Scott Thoms, photo editor

Photo Credit
Bruce Coleman Inc./Danilo Donadoni, 20–21

The author thanks the children's library staff at the Allen County Public Library in Fort Wayne, Indiana,
for research assistance.

Note to Parents and Teachers

The Dinosaurios y animales prehistóricos/Dinosaurs and Prehistoric Animals
set supports national science standards related to the evolution of life. This book
describes allosaurus in both English and Spanish. The images support early readers in
understanding the text. The repetition of words and phrases helps early readers learn
new words. This book also introduces early readers to subject-specific vocabulary words,
which are defined in the Glossary section. Early readers may need assistance to read
some words and to use the Table of Contents, Glossary, Internet Sites, and Index sections
of the book.

Table of Contents

Tabla de contenidos

A Strong Dinosaur

Allosaurus was a strong
dinosaur. It had a big head
with a bump over each eye.

Un dinosaurio muy fuerte

El alosaurio era un dinosaurio muy
fuerte. Tenía una cabeza grande y
un abultamiento encima de cada ojo.

Allosaurus lived

in prehistoric times.

It lived about

150 million years ago

in North America.

El alosaurio vivió en tiempos

prehistóricos. Vivió hace cerca

de 150 millones de años en

América del Norte.

How Allosaurus Looked

Allosaurus was about
as long as a fire truck.
It was about 38 feet
(12 meters) long.

Cómo eran los alosaurios

El alosaurio era tan largo
como un camión de bomberos.
Medía cerca de 12 metros
(38 pies) de largo.

Allosaurus had a long tail.
It held its tail off the ground
when it ran or walked.

El alosaurio tenía una larga
cola. Levantaba la cola
cuando corría o caminaba.

Allosaurus had long legs
and short arms.

El alosaurio tenía
las patas traseras largas
y las delanteras cortas.

What Allosaurus Did

Allosaurus hunted and ate other animals. It used sharp claws to kill other animals.

Qué hacían los alosaurios

El alosaurio cazaba y se comía a otros animales. Usaba sus afiladas garras para matar a otros animales.

Allosaurus bit its food.
Its teeth were sharp
and curved.

El alosaurio mordía
su comida. Sus dientes
eran filosos y curvos.

Allosaurus had a large,
strong mouth. It opened wide
to swallow food.

El alosaurio tenía una boca grande
y fuerte. La abría muy grande
para tragarse la comida.

The End of Allosaurus

Allosaurus died out about

135 million years ago.

No one knows why they all died.

You can see allosaurus fossils in museums.

El fin del alosaurio

El alosaurio desapareció hace cerca

de 135 millones de años. Nadie sabe

por qué todos murieron. Se pueden

ver fósiles de alosaurios en los museos.

Glossary

claw—a hard curved nail on the foot of an animal or a bird

dinosaur—a large reptile that lived on land in prehistoric times

fossil—the remains or traces of an animal or a plant, preserved as rock

hunt—to chase and kill animals for food

museum—a place where interesting objects of art, history, or science are shown

North America—the continent in the Western Hemisphere that includes the United States, Canada, Mexico, and Central America

prehistoric—very, very old; prehistoric means belonging to a time before history was written down.

Glosario

América del Norte—continente en el Hemisferio Occidental que incluye los Estados Unidos, Canadá, México y Centroamérica

cazar—perseguir y matar animales para comer

el dinosaurio—reptil grande de la prehistoria que vivía en tierra

el fósil—restos o vestigios de un animal o una planta que se conservan como piedras

la garra—uña dura y curva en la pata de un animal o un pájaro

el museo—lugar donde se exhiben objetos de arte, historia o ciencias

prehistórico—muy, muy viejo; prehistórico quiere decir perteneciente a una época antes de que hubiera historia escrita.

Internet Sites

FactHound offers a safe, fun way to find Internet sites related to this book. All of the sites on FactHound have been researched by our staff.

Here's how:

1. Visit *www.facthound.com*

2. Choose your grade level.

3. Type in this book ID **0736866833** for age-appropriate sites. You may also browse subjects by clicking on letters, or by clicking on pictures and words.

4. Click on the **Fetch It** button.

FactHound will fetch the best sites for you!

Index

ate, 14

body parts, 4, 10, 12, 14, 16, 18

claws, 14

died out, 20

dinosaur, 4

eye, 4

food, 14, 16, 18

fossils, 20

head, 4

hunted, 14

legs, 12

mouth, 18

museums, 20

North America, 6

prehistoric, 6

size, 8

tail, 10

teeth, 16

Sitios de Internet

FactHound proporciona una manera divertida y segura de encontrar sitios de Internet relacionados con este libro. Nuestro personal ha investigado todos los sitios de FactHound. Es posible que los sitios no estén en español.

Se hace así:

1. Visita *www.facthound.com*

2. Elige tu grado escolar.

3. Introduce este código especial **0736866833** para ver sitios apropiados según tu edad, o usa una palabra relacionada con este libro para hacer una búsqueda general.

4. Haz clic en el botón **Fetch It**.

¡FactHound buscará los mejores sitios para ti!

Índice

América del Norte, 6

boca, 18

cabeza, 4

cazaba, 14

cola, 10

comía, 14

comida, 14, 16, 18

desapareció, 20

dientes, 16

dinosaurio, 4

fósiles, 20

garras, 14

museos, 20

ojo, 4

partes del cuerpo, 4, 10, 12, 14, 16, 18

patas, 12

prehistóricos, 6

tamaño, 8